Clare and Bear

T0372066

Clare sits under the pear tree.
"I wish I had someone to play
with," she says.

Clomp! Clomp!

Clare hears footsteps nearby.

Clomp! Clomp!

"It's a bear! What's a bear
doing here?" thinks Clare.

"Hello, dear," says Bear.

"Hello, Bear," says Clare.

"Would you like to play
under our pear tree?"

Bear and Clare play under the pear tree.
"Would you care for morning tea?" says Clare.
Bear grins from ear to ear.
"Yes, that would be fantastic!"

Clare puts cake and milk on a square tray.

"You have a lot there," says Mum.

"Some for me and some for my friend, Bear," says Clare.

"That's good, dear," says Mum. "Have fun."

"A bear? A bear? Clare is going to share morning tea with a bear!" says Dad. "There's no time to spare," says Mum. "We'll snare the bear with a net!"

11

The garden is bare.
They look everywhere.
No bear! No Clare!
"I fear the bear has eaten
Clare," cries Mum.
Then Dad hears giggling.

13

"It would appear Bear is not a real bear," he says. "It's Miss Windermere from next door."

Mum and Dad laugh.
"Oh, Miss Windermere!
You gave us such a scare!"

Clare and Bear Level 7, Set 2a, Story 92

Words to blend

Clare	care	square
share	spare	bare
scare	bear	pear
there	everywhere	snare
giggling	eaten	fantastic
nearby	hello	garden

Clare and Bear

Before reading

Synopsis: Clare invites a friend to have some morning tea with her. But when Mum and Dad hear who it is, they are very alarmed!

Review phoneme and graphemes: /ear/ ere, eer

Focus phoneme: /air/ **Focus graphemes:** are, ear, ere

Story discussion: Look at the cover, and read the title together. Ask: *Who do you think Clare is? What is she doing? What do you think will happen in this book? Why?*

Link to prior learning: Remind children that the sound /air/ as in 'hair' can also be spelled 'are', 'ear' and 'ere'. Turn to page 8 and ask children to find a word with each spelling of the /air/ sound (Clare, square, bear, there).

Vocabulary check: snare: catch – 'We'll snare the bear with a net' means 'We'll catch the bear with a net'.

Decoding practice: Display the words 'everywhere', 'care', 'spare' and 'pear'. Can children circle the letter string that makes the /air/ sound, and read each word?

Tricky word practice: Display the word 'laugh'. Remind children that there are two tricky parts to this word – 'au', which makes the /ar/ sound (or /a/, depending on accent), and 'gh', which says /f/. Children could use the mnemonic 'Laugh at Uncle Greg's hat' to help them remember the spelling. Practise reading and writing this word.